T0365890

AUSTRALIA

A JOURNEY DOWN UNDER

KOLLIN L. TAYLOR

AuthorHouse™ LLC
1663 Liberty Drive
Bloomington, IN 47403
www.authorhouse.com
Phone: 1-800-839-8640

Published by AuthorHouse 10/30/2013

ISBN: 978-1-4918-2915-8 (sc)
*   978-1-4918-2928-8 (e)*

Library of Congress Control Number: 2013919679

Any people depicted in stock imagery provided by Thinkstock are models,
and such images are being used for illustrative purposes only.
Certain stock imagery © Thinkstock.

This book is printed on acid-free paper.

authorHOUSE®

AUSTRALIA

A JOURNEY DOWN UNDER

CONTENTS

Introduction

I went on a business trip to Australia in July, 2013. However, I knew the Lord had something in store for me. I knew He was going to put me to work: His work. When I went to Jamaica last December, I began writing poetry the day after I arrived. I felt that since I was going spend even more time in Australia, He was going to naturally inspire me to write about my experiences. I actually began working on this book while I was watching a movie on the flight to Brisbane, Australia. I was still about an hour away from landing when the creative juices started flowing.

I mentioned that God was going to put me to work, and He certainly did. I won't share the details in this book, but I will share one interesting fact from my walk with Him in Australia. I had a dream during my first night in Australia, on July 14, 2013. I dreamt that there were three people I was supposed to meet while I was there. I assumed they were supposed to shape my future. I don't recall what they looked like in the dream, but one was an aboriginal rugby player. I'm not sure if I remembered that one because it seemed the most improbable or because it was going to be the most significant. I'm here to testify that I met all three individuals within a twenty-four-hour period, between July 26, 2013 and July 27, 2013. The last person was not a rugby player, he was an aboriginal artist named Murruppi. He gave me permission to use his artwork for the cover page and throughout this book. If you are interested in learning more about him, aboriginal culture, and aboriginal art, visit www.murruppi.com. My trip to Australia would not have been complete without meeting an aborigine. I learned more about the country in five minutes from him than I learned in the previous two weeks.

Follow me on this journey Down Under to experience some of what Australia has to offer. I look forward to returning so I can see even more of this beautiful continent.

Note: The following book contains poetry with Australian lingo. Don't go to Australia and speak like that, because some Australians may have no idea what you're talking about.

Photo by Kollin L. Taylor

Connect with the author on Facebook at https://www.facebook.com/KollinLTaylor.

To the Australian Defence Forces, who hosted members of the US military during exercise Talisman Saber, 2013.

Acknowledgments

My Heavenly Father: Thanks for showing me that the things I can go out into the world and seek cannot compare to the things You deliver to me. One of the best gifts You've given to me is the ability to make a positive impact on the lives of people. Thanks for the opportunity to glorify your name on this incredible continent.

Jeremy (a.k.a. J. Sterm): You were my brother from another mother. Thanks for everything, especially for suggesting that I use Murruppi's artwork for the cover of this book; that was sheer brilliance, my friend.

Sterlin King: Thank you very much for your generosity; I'm eternally grateful.

Special Thanks

Murruppi: Thanks for your generosity. You shared your culture via music, art, and your words. You made my trip to Australia complete.

Connect with the author on Facebook at https://www.facebook.com/KollinLTaylor.

Southwest

It blew my mind as I flew south of the equator
And ended up Down Under a few days later.
The temperature got a bit colder,
And I got a few days older.

Traveling across the International Date Line
Took me forward in time.
Sailors who cross it on the sea
Celebrate with a special ceremony.

Photo by Kollin L. Taylor

Lost at Sea

This is a sad tale

About a humpback whale.

He made a very special sound,

And he wouldn't stop until his mate was found.

No one knows what drove them apart,

But everyone hears the sound of his heavy heart.

He will swim the oceans wide and blue

As his heartbeat says, "Where are you baby? I miss you."

Welcome Back Already

I haven't arrived yet, and I want to return one day,

And not for business but for a vacay.

I looked on the monitor in disbelief

When I saw the Great Barrier Reef.

I shivered as I thought about an infamous great white

And its notorious bite.

My honeymoon vision gave me a smile

When I saw a Fiji isle.

Sitting in the middle of the plane obscured my view,

But my next flight is going to include a view of you.

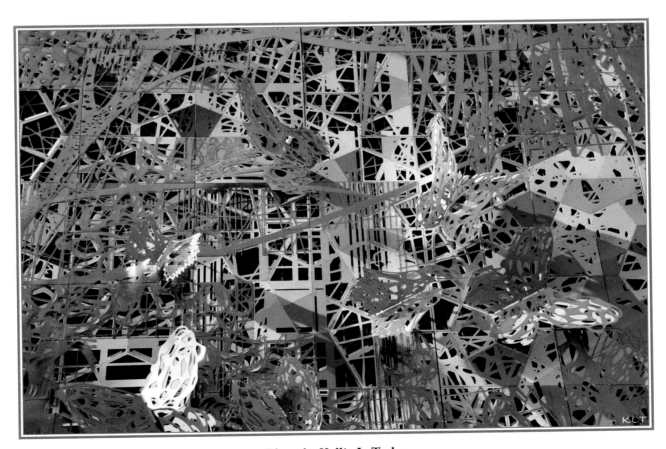

Photo by Kollin L. Taylor

Ayers Rock

The Father, Son, and the Holy Ghost went to a regalia
Down in the heart of Australia.
The continent filled them with so much zeal
That He created Ayers Rock, so they could have a meal.
They had angels prepare the meal and set the table,
And they used the clouds because they were able.
Now Ayers Rock is a part of Australian pride,
And it makes the Lord feel warm inside.

One Tonne

He went head over heels,
The kind a pain a person in the stands feels.
I thought it was the United States,
But he rolled out of Australian rodeo gates.

This man was no toy;
He was from the outback and a real cowboy.
He rode a bull called One Tonne,
Who bucked the cowboy and told him to run.
The cowboy refused to run away,
Because he knew he would tame the bull one day.

I thought I was back in the Midwest,
But instead I had witnessed Australia's best.

Joined at the Heart

In the middle of Brisbane, I heard a horn honk,
And on the radio I heard what sounded like honky-tonk.
One of the things about this Australian location
Is a country music station.

I know people go to Nashville, USA, to get big,
But I wonder how many come here for a country gig?
The United States and Australia are miles apart,
Yet they both have country music for your heart.

Australian Treasure

Handle with care:
I'm a cute and cuddly Koala Bear,
One of Australia's treasures to see,
Feasting in a eucalyptus tree.
I love the leaves, as you can tell,
With that potent medicinal smell.

Come on down and watch me play,
But I also sleep about twenty hours per day.

Photo by Kollin L. Taylor

Tasmanian Icon

From my size, you can't tell
That I'm the king of Tasmanian hell.
The devil is a title I deserve
For the mayhem that I serve.

Photo by Kollin L. Taylor

The Bush

There's one thing about being stush,
It makes life harder in the bush.
You don't have to worry about earthquakes,
But there're several poisonous snakes.

And take it from the insiders:
The bush also has several spiders.
There're several bugs that can give you the cruds,
But in the bush everyone's afraid of the floods.

I never thought I could swim a mile
Until that day I was chased by a crocodile.

Photo by Kollin L. Taylor

Pig 'n' Whistle

It wrapped around my lips like a thistle,
The incredible ribs from Pig 'n' Whistle.
In the middle of the Brisbane scene,
A British restaurant served an incredible cuisine.

It didn't take long, but it was worth the wait
To be served by an Irish lass named "Kate".
I ate too much and got out of control
In a sports bar where they let the good times roll.

There was a sign that asked "What's my beef?"
But I had none, to my relief.
Things got a bit loud, but not enough to make me deaf.
Then I had to compliment the chef.

The beef fell off the bones with ease,
But I'm too full, so no dessert, please.

Maroon and Blue

It's not time for fun or jokes;
There's a dividing line between lasses and blokes.
But the cause for this fender bender
Is not related to gender.
It may relate to the color on your face
But not as it relates to your race.

Everyone has to pick one of the two:
Either maroon or blue.
There's an explosion in ticket sales,
Because of the game between Queensland and New South Wales.

The field was filled with sweat, tears, and blood
From the hits that caused a crashing thud.
If you want to see someone who's proud,
Just look in the stands and check out the crowd.
But there're more fans than you can see,
All over the world listening to the radio or watching on TV.

Forty minutes and Queensland leads the score,
But the game still has at least forty minutes more.
But if you want to see the biggest bruise,
Just wait, because one of the teams will lose.

To gain an inch, the player fights,

Because the victor gets bragging rights.

The winning team's fans will cheer,

And the celebration will last more than a year.

They'll talk about this game for generations to come

And how gladiators came together in a scrum.

Ten points was New South Wales's final score,

But Queensland scored two points more.

But the highlight of the game was a fame-seeker,

And in case you missed it, they showed the male streaker.

Next year, the Blues will give it another go,

To try to stop the Mighty Maroons from making it nine in a row.

Note: Based on the 2013 Holden State of Origins rugby series.

Bush Doughnut

I'm as high as a kite,
Because a bush doughnut has me in flight.
There's so much that can be said
About jam between two slices of bread.

Oh yes, it's covered in pancake batter,
And cinnamon sugar tops this platter.

Slo-Mo

This may sound insane,
But have you ever seen slow-moving rain?
It almost looked cute;
Every raindrop had its own parachute.

I'm used to winter with falling snow,
But this Australian rain fell in slow-mo.
And then in about an hour,
It was a full-fledged rain shower.
I was reminded of the houses that were high,
Because they were on stilts to keep them dry.

The Lingo

The extent of the Australian lingo
Goes way beyond Wallaby and Dingo.
So before I say "hooroo,"
Here's what I'd like to do.
My pocket had "shrapnel" galore,
And "Makas" had a value meal for sure.
But the chill from the milkshake's sip
Caused me give a "fair crack of the whip".

Glossary:

Hooroo: good-bye
Makas: McDonald's
Shrapnel: coins of low value
Fair crack of the whip: to ease up

Aboriginal Tough

In life, we can pull or push,

And both describe life in the bush.

Things are so hard and remote;

It's hard to find a dingo with a shiny coat.

It can be a taste of hell

That wears on a Tasmanian Devil as well.

How can anything thrive

When it's hard enough to just survive?

Life in the bush is rough,

And a man has to be aboriginal tough.

With all the crocs, spiders, and snakes,

A survival instinct is what it takes.

When two predators fight,

It's because survival's a privilege and not a right.

But they won't fight all day long,

Because out in the bush you have to be smart and not just strong.

Artwork courtesy of Murruppi

Every Stride

I'm here to bear witness
That many Aussies love physical fitness.
It's not all about looking good,
But it's taking care of their bodies like they should.

Go to Brisbane and have some fun,
And you'll see thousands out for a walk, ride, or run.
I'm not sure if it's Aussie pride
That fuels every stride.

I just know it takes a lot of will
To tackle hill after hill.
The hills are so steep
That they'll make your legs weep.

But then you can relax and float,
And travel the river on a City Hopper boat.
And if you want to see an animal or two,
The Mirimar II will take you to a zoo.

Photo by Kollin L. Taylor

A Mile and a Smile

People in the city tend to have exteriors as cold as ice,

Even if their insides are county nice.

I walked through a park for about a mile

And broke the ice with "G'day" and a smile.

To say it always worked would be a lie,

But we'll never know if we never try.

Photo by Kollin L. Taylor

Shrapnel

Bigger isn't always better:
Just follow the number and letter.
An Aussie fifty-cent coin measures about an inch,
But a smaller one-dollar coin's worth more in a pinch.
And with loose change next to your loin,
You'll really want a two-dollar coin.

The coins paint a historic scene
By showing respect to the queen.
And just in case you're wondering who,
I'm referring to Britain's Queen Elizabeth II.

Capital City

While Sydney and Melbourne were in a fight,
Canberra earned the right
To be the country's capital city.
And to the losers, what a pity.

So while the other cities created a scene,
They chose the city that's between.

Penal Colony

If this was still a penal colony,

Dear Lord, sentence me here for an eternity.

But please do me a favor

And spare me the hard labour.

Photo of Story Bridge by Kollin L. Taylor

Reverse Migration

Now if you sail north of the Coral Sea,

You'll end up in Papua New Guinea.

People smugglers have something up their sleeve,

Because an Australian visa is not for everyone to receive.

So before anyone sets sail,

Ending up in PNG is an epic fail.

It means making a treacherous trip by sea,

With the intent to enter illegally.

The government implemented this drastic measure

So they can ask, "Are you here for business or pleasure?"

Illegal immigrants will take a toll

If they get beyond the country's control.

Law enforcement will have a hard time,

If entering the country is based on crime.

But here's one thing that's not lost on me:

People tried to leave when it was a penal colony.

Photo by Kollin L. Taylor

Talisman Saber

Can you please do me a favor
And tell me about Talisman Saber?
It's about covering the Pacific Ocean so blue
To partner with a friend, tried and true.

Whenever the enemy shook the rattle,
The Aussies always joined the battle.
To win you have to dare,
And to partner you have to share.

But just in case the enemy decides to push,
The US stands ready to join the Aussies in the bush.
Even though the Aussies have their plan,
The US will try to do what they can.

But for people to travel this far,
This exercise is about more than war.
Like after a battle's mess is made,
People will need help from groups like AusAID.

And as we partner through weeks of strife,
We'll make friends for life.
As we practice things in every aspect,
We leave as friends, bound by mutual respect.

Life's Bend

I threw it away as hard as I could,

But it returned like it should.

From the beginning to the end,

Life's a boomerang with edges and a bend.

An instrument of peace and war,

It's a friend who leaves but never goes far.

A boomerang comes in different shapes and sizes,

And, like life, it's full of surprises.

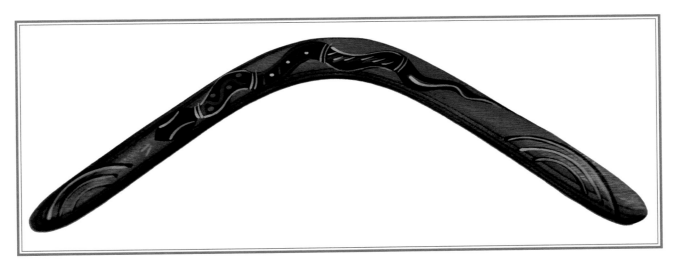

Boomerang by Murruppi

Continental Tour

Adelaide sings,
Which gave Alice Springs.
Gladstone and Rock Hampton are not crocs,
But Ayers is truly a rock.

There're great white sharks at the Great Barrier Reef,
But to the fish and people, that's no relief.
Is there a surfboard within reach?
Because I'm heading down to Mona Vale Beach.

A trip to Sidney is of worth,
And so are going to Darwin and Perth.
There're succulent grapes, growing on vines,
That get fermented to make Australia's best wines.

There's so much more to see
Of this wonderfully diverse country.

Photo by Kollin L. Taylor

Dingo Line

We know what you sow is what you reap.

The Aussies sowed a fence to protect the sheep.

Australia has the world's longest fence,

Because things between the sheep and dingoes got tense.

The dingoes walk the line and continue to probe,

And the sheep are on edge with a radar-like earlobe.

Terror of the Night

What in the heck was that?
It cast a shadow like a megabat.
It sounded like a beagle,
But it had a wingspan like an eagle.

It filled even the brave with fright
And brought terror to the night.
But during the day, it can be found
Sleeping away and hanging around.

Either way, this bat rocks—
A terror in the sky called the Flying Fox.
But blood is not its loot,
Because it only craves the juices from a fruit.

Flying Monkey

I thought a monkey was in a tree,

Laughing hysterically at me.

But it had wings and a beak the size of a bloke

And sounded like a monkey whenever it spoke.

A Kookaburra is a sight to see,

But you need to hear this bird that sounds like a monkey.

Pink Suit

Hey! How are you,

Oh beautiful, wild cockatoo?

It was wilder than you'd think,

With a breastplate covered in pink.

It was a beautiful sight,

Both while perched and in flight.

The bird was loud yet cute,

And it looked dapper in its feathery suit.

Red, Black, and Gold

Oh my! What the heck?
Was that a black turkey with a red neck?
It was a cute little fellow,
With vertical tail feathers and a beard in yellow.

I saw it run away in fright
As a kookaburra put up a fight.
The turkey's head was already covered in red,
Which made the kookaburra target its head.

The turkey wasn't gifted with flight,
But it ran into the bush and disappeared like it was night.

Photo by Kollin L. Taylor

Saint or Sinister

There is politics,

And then there are poly tricks.

Some things a country's leader will fix

And yet still get beaten with verbal sticks.

Regardless of his political rating,

The Australian Prime Minister will get served with lots of hating.

Whether a saint or someone sinister,

There's a lot of pressure in the role of prime minister.

Near-Drowning

Billabong is an icon that almost went down,
But that would be like letting a great white shark drown.
It took a deal worth over three hundred mil
To serve as the company's magic pill.

Billabong is of Australian birth,
But it's an icon all over the earth.

Test Match

I'm broadcasting live from the ticket,

An oval with a pitch for the game of cricket.

It's in the heat of the day,

With two batsmen on a pitch of pressed clay.

The Brits put up a three-hundred-run score,

And to win, the Aussies only need one point more.

The Aussies have scored two hundred fifty runs with nine.

They only have one more out, but the fans think they'll do just fine.

The game will rapidly go south

If the Brits get another one out.

The field has two Aussie men,

Against the Brits' eleven.

The game is a gut-wrenching race,

And the Brits change from a spin bowler to a fast pace.

The bowler is taller than a garden house,

As he shines up the ball by rubbing it on his clothes.

He then uses a special grip

And runs with the ball on a bouncing trip.

He swings his arm high above his shoulder

And delivers the red ball like a speeding boulder.

The batsman was blessed with luck

When he decided to duck.

When the ball hit the ground,

It leapt over his head in one big bound.

The batsman almost met the grim reaper,

But instead the ball was caught by the wicket keeper.

The bowler went back and marked off his pace

And then took off running on another race.

This time when the ball left the ground,

The swing of the bat made that sound.

The batsman hit the ball with all of his might,

And the ball took off on an incredible flight.

Into the stands, the ball soared,

And that resulted in six runs scored.

The bowler's heart filled with steam,

Even though he was encouraged by his team.

He went back to his starting line

And took off running with the ball another time.

Again, the batsman did just fine

By scoring four runs by hitting the ball on the ground to the boundary line.

The bowler had a determined look on his face.

He wanted to hit those wickets behind the batsman all over the place.

The batsman's swing of the bat was clipped;

It fell into the slip, but the fielder tripped.

The Brits in the stands had faces of death

While an Aussie passed out from holding her breath.

The bowler was experiencing pure misery,

As he made another valiant delivery.

The batsman hit the ball by the bowler's face,

And the ball rolled toward the boundary at a face pace.

Scoring four more runs was a need,

But the ball was stopped by a fielder with incredible speed.

The batsmen's muscles started to twitch,

As they ran to score points at the other end of the pitch.

The Aussie fans' spirits soared,

Even though only one run was scored.

The game was nowhere near done;

The Aussies kept scoring run after run.

I won't update the score

Except to say that the Aussies scored many runs more.

This game wasn't just a match; it was a test

To see which team was among the world's best.

But, at the end of the day,

One country was happy, and the other was in dismay.

The sweetness of victory and the agony of defeat

Will follow the teams until the next time they meet.

For baseball fans who don't understand the game,

I hope this showed they're almost the same.

Both have eleven players governed by rules,

With bats and balls among their tools.

Before I bid this game adieu,

Let me say that ladies play cricket, too.

The rules are the same as for the lads,

To include batters wearing thick gloves and leg pads.

And the one thing that always stuns:

When a batsman scores more than a hundred runs.

"Budgy Smugglers"

Get "cashed up" before making this trip,

And wear your "budgy smugglers" when the waves rip.

Give surfing a "burl" if you go to the beach,

And "by crickey" may become a part of your speech.

Sure you could "cark"

If you encounter a shark.

But you won't come all this way

Without having some excitement every day.

Glossary:

Budgy smugglers or togs: swimwear

Give it a burl: give it a go

By crickey: an expression of surprise

Cark it: to die

Cash up: having plenty of ready money

Photo by Kollin L. Taylor

41

Iconic Meat

The menu almost knocked me off my seat
When I saw that they served kangaroo meat.
Killing such an icon may sound mean,
But compared to beef or lamb, the meat's real lean.

I didn't have kangaroo meat on my placemat,
But some may be tempted, since it's only 1 to 2 percent fat.

Photo by Kollin L. Taylor

Aboriginal Art

Where do I start?!
There's something special about aboriginal art.
These aren't things that are only in caves,
And their beauty causes shockwaves.

They paint beautiful things that tug at the heart,
Like koalas, snakes, and wallabies getting off to a running start.
Some things look like colorful sponge dabs,
And others are crisscrossed on slabs.

And it was like pointillism, where dots abound,
On a didgeridoo with its beautiful resonant sound.

Artwork courtesy of Murruppi

ADCU

How does this trip rank?

It's all based on the bank.

Specifically, the ADCU*,

Where I received a friendly smile or two.

Thanks, ladies, for brightening my day

And for your support along the way.

*Australian Defence Credit Union

The Streets

I did an experiment in the street,
Because with a smile I would greet
People along the way.
But most people didn't give me the time of day.

I walked down the street real proud,
And I said, "Good morning," clear and loud.
But most of the time when I said, "Hi,"
People silently walked by.

You can just imagine how that made me feel,
As it made this country lose its appeal.
But people in the world's cities usually have rust
That makes them view others with distrust.

But whenever I sat down to eat,
The servers were willing to greet.
But their service had a different flare,
Maybe because tipping isn't common here.
But a server can help make a person's day,
And for that I'm willing to pay.

Now back to my city walk
Along the river and my attempts to talk.
Every once in a while,
Someone reciprocated a friendly greeting and smile.
But if I had waited,
It seemed as if no one would've initiated.

Despite my apparent invisibility,
Some had it even worse than me.
I saw something that almost made me weep,
When I saw some homeless people asleep.

Two were young, and one was old,
And being homeless made life extra cold.
I dared not assume their affliction
Was because of some form of addiction.

I later saw two of them pushing shopping carts along the way,
So I smiled and gave the greeting of the day.
I went on this walk, because I felt my life was a mess,
And I needed time to cry and decompress.
But when I thought I had it rough,
I saw some people who had to be tough.

They didn't make me feel better.
Instead, they made my eyes get wetter.
Their challenges didn't make my life seem great,
Because suffering is something I hate.

I could've helped in so many ways,
But I could've only helped for a few days.
It seemed almost cruel to offer a warm shower
And put them back in the street the next hour.

But my experiences on this big city street
Were typical for most cities and the people you meet.
This morning was an incredible start to the day,
And for the world's homeless I pray.

Photo by Kollin L. Taylor

ADF

Thanks to the ADF* for your hospitality
And for making this trip a pleasant memory.
Even though I couldn't have wine,
I appreciated the opportunity to dine.
You provided meals in the dining facility
With pleasant workers like Marie.

And then there was a good feeling that lasted for a while,
Thanks to Lauren and her friendly smile.
The truth is I wasn't having my best day,
And you showed that a friendly smile goes a long way.

*The Australian Defence Force

Photo by Kollin L. Taylor

Ned Kelly

You have to be as "game as Ned Kelly,"

To pet a gator on its belly.

Because you can't say, "Don't get off your bike"

When it gets angry and shows you why they call it spike.

Glossary:

Don't get off your bike: calm down

Glutton

Whether an ewe or a ram,

I'm a glutton for lamb.

And speaking of glutton,

A lamb's meat is called mutton.

Relative Obscurity

It seems as if no one remembers me;

I'm but a poor wallaby.

Everyone makes a hullabaloo

About my relative the kangaroo.

But without fail,

We both have a powerful tail.

One kick will make you say, "Ouch!"

We even both carry our babies in a pouch.

Yes, we're a little smaller,

And they stand taller.

But, it's apparent to me

That we're still family.

Photo by Kollin L. Taylor

Murruppi

I can't believe how this started.

Murruppi, thanks for the knowledge you imparted.

It was a pleasure meeting you

And learning about the didgeridoo.

Thanks for breaking it down

By explaining the meaning of the sound.

You made it sound like a dove's coo

And the leaping kangaroo.

You shared some interesting facts,

Like how it's made from a eucalyptus tree and tipped with beeswax.

You told me about the wild bees that do not sting

And how it was hollowed out by termites feasting.

The instrument does not sound like a typical symphony,

But it's a perfect blend of man and Mother Nature to me.

So again, Murruppi, thanks from the bottom of my heart

For sharing your aboriginal sounds and art.

As this trip comes to an end,

Cheers, my friend!

Note: I'm sure you guessed it, but the above poem was inspired by an aboriginal artist I met in Australia named Murruppi. He was gracious enough to donate the images that were used for the cover and throughout this book. If you're interested in learning more about him or aboriginal culture, visit www.murruppi.com.

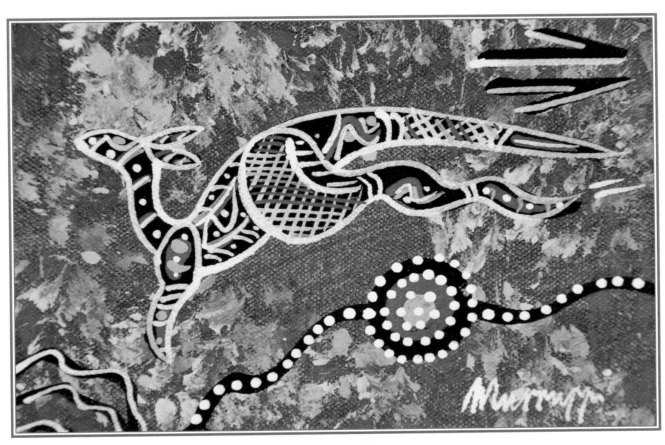

Artwork courtesy of Murruppi

ABOUT THE AUTHOR

Kollin L. Taylor went through a heartbreaking situation that brought him closer to God (his ultimate source of inspiration) and launched his writing career as an author and poet as a way to deal with the pain. He started off by writing the narrative The Anatomy of a Heartbreak—When SAMson met Delilah but was inspired to write poetry in the middle of writing that book. In the last twelve months, he was inspired to write enough material for thirty-eight books, more than twelve hundred poems. While he hopes others do not get into writing the way he did, he bravely shares some of his inspired works in the following books:

Exposed, Part I: The Prelude
Exposed, Part II: Romantic Relationships
Exposed, Part III: Vida
Exposed Part IV:⊠.. The Journey Continues
Metamorphosis: The New Me
The Phenom: From My Soul
Resilience: Bend, Don't Break
The Aftermath: When the Smoke Clears & the Dust Settles
Perspective: A New Point of View
The Anatomy of a Heartbreak: When SAMson met Delilah (narrative)
Round 2: The Battle Continues
Round 3: Still Fighting
Cool Breeze: Irie Man
Finding Joy in YOU: The Gift of Eternal Life
Minister to the People: Answering His Calling
The Path to Enlightenment
Australia: A Journey Down Under is his seventeenth book, and his sixteenth book of poetry.

Author photo by Sterlin King

Connect with the author on Facebook at https://www.facebook.com/KollinLTaylor.

Printed in the United States
By Bookmasters